INTRODUCTIC

We have completed this compreher..... ....mvo

to call your cat or kitten while at the peak of the

COVID-19 Pandemic and its Variants.

We thought it would be a good idea to produce a

comprehensive book of over 1001 names, which will

inspire you to choose one for your furry friend, some

names are with definitions.

We want to try and bring peace happiness and joy
in helping you to decide on a name your furry friend.

I want to thank Beryl Dowson, my mother, Jan

Webber my sister who is a children's author in her own

right and Rachael O 'Connell my partner in contributing

names for this book.

David Dowson.

www.daviddowson.com.

I hope you enjoy this book and that it gives you inspiration.

David Dowson who is an established author of the book The Path of a Chess Amateur an updated chess book will be published soon. He is a retired cryptographer from GCHQ UK.

David is a Tae Kwon do master as well as a trained Classical Artist

He is also a Professional Photographer of Landscapes, Wildlife, Portraits, Weddings etc.

A

Amender

Amy

Andrea

Andrea

Angel

Anita

Ann

Anna

Ambrose

immortal. Greek in
origin.

Annabelle

Annie

Anny

Apple

Apricot

April

From the Latin to
open.

Arch

Archi

Archie

Ardie

Aris

Aristotle

Arnie

Arthur

Ashburn

Ashton

Aslan

Aspen

Aspin

Aster

Astra

Ava

Avery
Ace

The aces of spades
and clubs are black
and white.

Ajax

One of the Greek
heroes of the Trojan
war

B

Babe

Babs	Bell
Baby	Bella
Bagel	Ben
Bailey	Bennie
Bally	Benson
Banded	Bentley
Bandit	Berkeley
Barbie	Berry
Barbosa	Bertie
Barbra	Betty
Barclay	Bianca
Barkley	Bianca
Barton	Billy
Bash	Billy boy
Bear	Bingo
Beasley	Binky
Beatrix	Bippy
Becky	Birdie
Belinda	Biscuit

Bisha	Bosch
BJ	Brace
Blackie	Bracket
Blaze	Brad
Blender	Bradley
blossom	Branded
Blossom	Brenda
Blue	Bria
Bluebell	Brian
Bluey	Bridget
Bob	Brooklyn
Bobby	Brutus
Bojo	Bubble
Bonney	Buckley's
Bonnie	Buddha
Bonobo	Buddy
Bonza	Bunny
Boo	Buster
Boomer	Butchered

Butter cup

Butter scotch

Buttercup

Button

Buttons

Byron

C

Cabbage

Caesar

Caissa

Calvin

Camellia

Camping

candy

Candy	Charlotte
Canon	Chasey
Carissa	Checkers
Carmen	Cheerio
Carrel	Chelsea
Carrie	Chenie
Carrion	cherries
Carrol	Cherry
Carter	Cheryl
Cassandra	Chevy
Cassia	Chinx
Cassis	Chloe
Catrina	Chocolate
Cecil	Christian
Chaka	Christine
Chapple	Christopher
Charlene	Christy
Charley	Churchill
Charlie	Cider

Cilla	Colette
Cinder	collect
Cinders	Coping
Cindy	Corey
Clare	Corky
clarence	Cortina
Claudia	Crab
Clear	Creed
Clementine	Crimbo
Cleo	Cristal
Cleopatra	Cristy
Clove	Cromwell
Clover	Cruiser
Coco	Crystal
Cody	Cuddle
Coffee	Cuddles
Coffey	Cue tip
Cola	Cupid
Colby	Custard

Cynthia

Cyrus

D

D'artagnan

Daffy

Daisy

Daisy

Dakota

Dalton

Dan

Dana

Daniel

Danielle

Dara

Darla

Darling

Dave	Diesel
Dawn	Dilly
Deanna	Dimond
Debbie	Dinah
Deck	diner
Deena	Dinho
Defies	Dinky
Delboy	Dipsy
Delia	Districting
Delilah	Dixie
Delray	Django
Demah	Dobbin
Denude	Dobbs
Desire	Dolly
Dessie	Dolly
Destiny	Domino
Diamond	Donna
Diana	Doodles
Dianne	Dora

Doris	
Dot	E
Dotti	Earnie
Dottie	Ebony
Dotty	Echo
Doug	Edal
Douglas	Edie
Duke	Edna
Dusty	Edwina
	Eggy
	Eileen
	Elbow
	Elder
	Elea
	Eleanor
	Elf
	Elizabeth
	Elkader
	Ellen

Ellery

Ellie

Elsa

Elvis

Emery

Emily

Emma

Emmer

Erica

Espresso

Essie

Ester

Ethel

Eustace

Eva

Eve

Evie

Expresso

F

Fabio

Face

facial

Fae

fanny

Farid

fay

Feeney

Felicity

Fenton

Fergus

Fidget

Fifi

Figgie

Filbert

Finny

Fiona

Flipper

Flo

Floppy

Flora

Florence

Florida

Florrie

Flower

Flower

Fluffy

Foxtrot

Foxy

Francis

Frankie

Franny

Freckles

Frisky

Frizzy

Frosty

funny

Furball

Fuzz

Fuzzy

Gandalf

Ganger

Geno

Gentle

Geoff

George

Gertrude

Giles

Gillie

Ginger

Ginger

Gizmo

Glenda

Glendora

G

Gloria

Gabby

Goldie

Gabriel

Google

Gail

Gordon

Gala

Gouda

Gracie

Gravy

Gray

Greta

Grumpy

Guy

Gypsy

H

Haden

Hallie

Hamish

Hampton

Hank

Hanna

Hans

Happy

Harley

Harold

Harper

Harriet

Harry

Harvey

Havana

Hawkins

Hazel

Heath

Heath cliff

Heather

Heather

Heidi

Helena

Helga

Henrietta

Henry

Hensley

Herbert

Herbie

Herby

Hero

Hershey

Hesper

Hester

Higgins

Higley

Hihi

Hillary

Hinton

Hippie

Hippy

Holby

Holly

Honda

Honey

Honker

Hope

Horatio

Hosp

Hosta

Hostel

Howard

Howie

Hubert

Hunk

Hunt

Hunter

I

Ian

Iasha

Ida

Ike

India

Indigo

Ingrid

inky

Irene

Iris

Irish

Irvin

Irwin

Isaac

Isabel

Isabella

Isabelle

Ives

ivory

Ivory

Ivy

Iwana

Izzy

J

Jack

Jackey

Jackie

Jacob

Jacqueline

Jada

Jadi

James

Jamie

Jane

Janet

Janice

Janie

Janna

Jasmin

Jasmine

Jason

jasper

Java

Jayne

Jazz

Jazzy

Jean

Jeanie

Jeff

Jenny

Jerry

Jesper

Jessica

Jessie

Jessop

Jester	john
Jesus	Johnny
Jewel	JoJo
Jezebel	Jolene
Jigsaw	Jolie
Jill	Jonah
Jillian	Joni
jimbe	Jorden
Jimmy	Jordi
Jingles	Joseph
Jinks	Josephine
jives	Joshua
JJ	Josie
Joanie	Joy
Joann	Joyce
Jodi	Judy
Jody	Jules
Joe	Julia
Joey	Julie

Juliet

July

Jumbo

Jumbo

Jumper

June

jungle

Juniper

Justin

K

Kai	Kellie
Kale	Kelly
Kaley	Kelsey
Kalie	Kendal
Kara	kendo
Karen	Kenya
Kassie	Key
Kate	kibbles
Katerina	Kimble
Kathie	Kinga
Kathy	Kirby
Katie	Kirk
Katye	Kirsty
Katye	Kissy
Kea	Kit kat
Keisha	Kitty
Keith	Kramer
Keith	Kyrton

L

Lacey

Lacy

Lady

Laine	Loki
Lauren	Lola
Laurie	Loretta
Lavender	Lorna
Lee	Loti
Lena	Lottie
Leno	Louis
Leo	Louise
Lettie	Lucas
Lexi	Lucey
Libby	Lucie
Lilac	Lucky
Lily	Lucy
Linda	Luke
Lindahl	Lulu
Lister	Luna
Lizzy	Lynn
Lock	
Lois	

M

Macey

Maddie

Madeline

Madison

Maggie

Mama

Mambo

Mandy	Mathew
Manikin	Matilda
Marbella	Maurice
Marcia	Mavis
Marcus	Max
Margaret	Maxi
Margarita	Maxie
Margie	Maxine
Marianne	May
Marilyn	mCharity
Marina	Megan
Mark	Meki
Marla	Melanie
Marley	Melody
Marlo	Melvin
Marmite	Mia
Mary	Michael
Mason	Mildred
Massa	Mile

Millie	Morgan
Milo	Morris
Mina	Moses
Mincey	Mumbai
Mindy	Mustard
Minecraft	Mustard
Minna	Myra
Minnie	N
Minx	Nacho
Mira	Nada
Miranda	Nally
Misha	Nancey
Miss Tibbs	Nancy
Missy	Nanna
Mo	Natasha
Molly	Nathan
Monkey	Naughty
Moon	Ned
Mopey	Neddie

Needles

Neil

Nellie

Nero

Nibble

Nibs

Nickel

Nicol

Nicolas

Nicole

Nicoleta

Nike

Niki

Nikki

Niles

Nimble

Nina

Ninja

Noah

Nobel

Noel

Nora

Noreen

Norma

Norman

Norris

Nova

O

Oakey

Oakley

Okie

Olive

Olivia

Olivier

Ollie

Onyx

Opal

Oreo

Oscar

Owen

P

Paddy

Pamela

Panda

Panking

Pansy

Paris

Parise

Patch

Patra

Patsey

Patsy

Pattie

Patty

Patullos

Paws

Payton

Peaches

Peanut	Pilgrim
Peewee	Pilot
Peggy	Pineapple
Penha	Ping
Penny	pinkie
Pepper	Pinkie
perky	Pino
Pester	Pippa
Peta	Pippin
Petal	Pistachio
Peter	Pistuehi
Petra	Pixel
Pettle	Pixie
Philo	Pock
Phoenix	pokey
Phono	Polly
Pickle	Pollyanna
Piece	Ponca
Pierre	Pong

Pooch

Poodle

Pookie

Popactapl

Popeye

Poppet

Poppy

Porky

Possie

Potty

pressure

prier

Primrose

Prince

Princes

Prudence

Puddles

Puffin

Puffy

Pumpkin

Punky

Purr

Pussy

Quin

Quincey

Quinn

Quinton

Quiverer

Q

Quaker

Queenie

Queeny

Quibbled

Rand

Randy

Ranger

Rascal

Rascal

Rashford

Raspberry

Raspier

Raspier

Reg

Rene

Rex

R   Rhubarb

R 2 D 2   Ribbon

Rachael   Richard

Rah Rah   Rickey

Ralph   Ricky

Rambo   Rider

Ramee   Riley

Ripley

Rita

Robbie

Robbin

Robert

Robin

Rocky

Rodger

Rollo

Roman

Ronald

Ronnie

Rooney

Rosana

Rosco

Rose

Rosemary

Rosey

Rosie

Roxio

Roy

Ruby

Runcie

Runco

Rusty

Ruth

Ruthie

S

Sabrina

Sadie

Saffron

Sagan

Sage

Sally

Salvatore

Sam

Sam

Samantha

Sammie

Sampson

Samsung

Samuel

Sand

Sandy

Santa

Sara

Sassy

Sausage

Selena

Sha

Shake

Sheba

Sheila

Shelly

Sherley

Sherry

Shinder

Shining	smooch
Shirly	Smudge
Shrew	Sniffer
Siam	sniffles
Sid Vicious	Snippy
Silky	Snoopy
Silvester	Snowdrop
Silvia	Snowy
Simba	Sol
Simon	Sony
Sissy	Sophie
Skip	Sophy
Skipper	Spam
Sky	Spanner
Slavic	Sparky
Slipper	Spik
Smarty	Spike
Smokey	Spitfire
Smokey	Spotty

Star

Stedman

Stella

Stevie

Stiles

Storm

Strawberry

Sue

Sugar

Sullivan

Summer

Sunny

Susan

Susanna

Susie

Suzuki

Sylvia

Syrus

T

Tabby

Tabs

Tanya

Tara

Tasha

Tealeaf

Tegula

Television

Terry

Tesco

Tess

Tessa

Tessie

Thelma

Thinking

Thyme

Tia

Tiara

Tibbey

Tibbs

Tiger

Tiger Lilly

Tillie

TILLY

Time

Timmy

Tina

Tinkerbell

Titan

Todd

Tom

Tonja

Tony

Tootie

Topsy

Troy

Trudy

Tucker

Tusk

Tussles

Twiggy

Twinkle

Tyler

Tyson

U

ultra

Uranus

Urban

Ursula

V

Vance

Vandal

Vanilla

Veera

Venue

Venus

Vera

Veronica

Vester

Vickie

Victoria

Vincent

Vinny

Viola

Virgil

Vivian

Vixen

W

Walter

Wanda

Wander

Wayne

Wendy

Wester

Westley

Whiskers

Whitney

Whoopy

Wilder

William

Willis

willow

Wilma

Winnie

X

Xenia

Xerox

Y

Yale

Yellow

Yoke

Yule

Yvette

Yvonne

Z

Zakk

Zaza

Zebra

Zelda

Zelma

Zhan

Zia

Zilly

Zoe

Zoran

Zornia

Zoya

Zulu

Abby

Abby means "joy of the father,"

Adam

Means son of the read earth.

Adrian

Meaning SEA or WATER

Alannah

The meaning is for beauty or serenity.

Alaska

It derives from the word ALAXSXQA meaning mainland.

Alex

This word is Greek in origin, and the meaning is managed defender warrior.

Alexa

Meaning of this word. Is defender of man?

Alexander

Meaning of this word. Is defender of men? Mostly famous associated with Alexander the Great.

Alfie

Alfie is a boy's name. It is an old English. and German origin meaning elf or magical being.

Alice

Is a girl's name of German origin, meaning noble?

Allan

Alan is the name meaning popularity and info on baby names.

Aloe

is a succulent plant? Chiefly southern African. Plants of the Lily family.

Amanda

Is a Latin name, meaning lovable or worthy of love?

Amber

Amber is from discussed Sanskrit word meaning A gemstone that is a yellow-orange colour. By mother in this case is used mainly Hindi parents.

Alabaster
A type of stone (like marble).

Alex

It' means "defender of men" in Greek.

Alexander Puss-kin

Alexander Pushkin famous Russian poet and novelist.

Ali

One meaning of Ali is "noble,"

Alonzo

One meaning is "ready for battle,"

Angel

A spiritual being superior to humans in power and intelligence.
Annie
Means Gracious, Merciful, Diminutive form of Ann(e)

Like the character in the musical "Annie,"

Apple Jack

Is your cat orange like cider?

Arabella

It's a name favoured by British novelists like Thomas Hardy and J.K. Rowling,

Archie

One meaning of Archie is "truly bold," also prince William and Kate named their son.

Artemis

Greek Goddess.

Ash or Ashley

Because ashes are grey in colour.

Athena

Cats are wise, so taking a name from the Greek goddess of wisdom and war makes.

Atlas

From Greek mythology, Atlas is the god who held the weight of the world on his shoulders.

Babe

After the film "Babe?"

Baby

An affectionate form of address.

Bagheera

From the fictional character from the JUNGLE BOOK.

Baguette

This name for a long loaf of bread.

Bahia

This state in Brazil is known for its laid-back vibe, beaches, and as the birthplace of the samba. (Or just call her) Samba.

Bambino

This means "little child" or "baby" in Italian!

Beans

Full of beans means lots of energy

Bear

A good cat name for any cat that resembles a teddy bear.

Beckham

Name of footballer David Beckham.

Bella

The name means "beautiful" in Italian and Spanish.

Belle

Belle means "beauty" in French.

Beltza

This is the word for "black" in the Basque language, but

Berlioz

This is the Disney cat name belonging to the grey kitten who plays the piano in the movie "The Artistocats."

Biggs

After Ronnie Biggs UK great train robber.

Binx

Thackery Binx is the name of the cat in the Halloween classic, "Hocus Pocus."

Biscuit

This after a biscuit (cookie) as its SWEET to the tast.

Blanca or Blanco

The Spanish words for "white." Blanca is a female cat name, while Blanco is a boy's cat name

Blanche

The French word for "white."

Blue

Inspired by Beyonce and Jay-Z's daughter, Blue Ivy. Can also be spelled Bleu or Blu.

Bob

A classic human name, as in the book called a cat maned BOB.

Bolt

A cat that can run as fast as Usain Bolt?

Boo

B00 is defined as a word of endearment between girlfriend and boyfriend also used to disapprove of something.

Boots

Named after Puss in Boots who is Shrek's sidekick.

Bowser

Inspired by "King Koopa" from Super Mario.

Brady

From the Brady Bunch, Brady can be a good male cat name.

Briggs

This English surname would make a unique cat name.

Brooklyn

The New York City borough known for its hipster culture.

Brownie

After a cake.

Bubbles

A thin sphere of
soap that floats
then bursts.

Buddy

For your best
friend.

Buttercup

The pet of Primrose
Everdeen in "The
Hunger Games."
Also, a yellow
flower.

Butterscotch

A sweet (candy)
loved by all.

Button

As bright as a Button.
To be cleaver.

Buster

After the great train
robber UK.

Calvin

Inspired by the
comic strip, "Calvin
and Hobbes."
Calvin is the
adventurous six-
year-old boy.

Cantaloupe

This could be a
funny cat name for
an orange cat.

Cara

Cara navel oranges found in Venezuela.

Casper

Mainly for white cats from Casper the friendly Ghost.

Cassie

Short for Cassandra.

Cat Winslet

After actress Kate Winslet.

Catrina

A play on the name Katrina.

Chaka Khat

In honour of the one and only Chaka Khan.

Charlie

Charlie is a popular name among people and pets and means "free man."

Checkers

Checkerboards are often black and white, just like a black-and-white cat.

Chloe

A Greek name connected to the goddess Demeter, Chloe is one of the most popular cat name.

Cho Chang

"Harry Potter," you'll recognize this name as a Ravenclaw, Quidditch player, and Harry's girlfriend.

Claudia.

A play on the name Claudia Winkleman.

Clementine

Hybrid oranges make a great cat name.

Cleo

Short for "Cleopatra," Egyptian ruler.

Clyde

Name inspired by the infamous criminal couple Bonnie and Clyde.

Coco

Short for coconut.

Cocoa

A cute cat name for a brown kitten.

Cricket

Name inspired by personality trait of meowing loudly at 2 a.m.!

Crookshanks

The name of Hermione Granger's cat, from the "Harry Potter" series.

Daisy

Another flower name that is a pretty for a cat.

Dinah

The cat who belongs to Alice in "Alice in Wonderland."

Dipsy

One of the Teletubbies.

Dobby

The house elf from "Harry Potter."

Dolly

Dolly is a cart with two wheels and long handles used for moving heavy objects.

Domino

These tiles are black and white, so why not chose this for your black-and-white cat?

Dot

Polka dots are often black and white, for your cat!

Dottie

Another name for "Dot," which means "gift of God."

Draco

Draco Malfoy is not a sympathetic character in "Harry Potter," but the name is a great one for a cat.

Duchess

The mother of Berlioz, Toulouse and Marie in "The Artistocats."

Ducky

Ducky is a British way of saying someone or something is " "cute."

Dusk

Right before night begins, the sky is a shade of grey – just like your cat.

Ebony

Referring to a tree with black or very dark brown wood, the word is now used as a synonym for black.

Einstein

Convinced your cat is a genius? Well, this is the name for you!

Ella

Ella Fitzgerald, the great jazz artist,

was known for her improvised scat singing.
makes a great name!

Emma

Emma Thompson is a British actress with a keen sense of humour.

Fat Louie

The cat belonging to Anne Hathaway's character in "The Princess Diaries" (2001).

Fawkes

The name of Dumbledore's phoenix in the "Harry Potter" series could also be used for your cat. Also Guy Fawkes who attempted to blow up parliament.

Figaro

The black-and-white pet cat who belongs to Geppetto in "Pinocchio."

Figgy

After figgy pudding, a dessert that also goes by the name of plum or Christmas pudding. it's a cake, soaked in rum or brandy.

Fiona

The origin of Fiona is Scottish, and it

means "white" or "fair."

Fitz

This is a name derived from last names (Fitzgerald, Fitzwilliam) but it's short and sweet, like your cat.

Fleur

A "Harry Potter"-inspired cat name that comes from Fleur Delacour, who was Beauxbatons' champion in the Triwizard Tournament.

Fluffy

A long-fluffy haired cat.

Frank

A classic human name can make for a great male cat name!

Frankie

If you're looking for great unisex cat name ideas, Frankie is a great option.

Fraser

Was a famous TV character.

Frosty

From frosty the snowman, when frost covers the ground, it turns the grass a ghostly shade of white.

Furry Elise

"Fur Elise" might be one of Beethoven's best-known piano pieces, beloved at student piano recitals everywhere.

Gaia

The ancient Greeks considered Gaia to be Mother Earth, so this is the name for you.

Gary

Gelato

Sure, gelato is an Italian frozen dessert.

George

The name George means "farmer," which could be a fitting name for the cat that lives on a farm.

Ginger

Another word for redheads, both male and female.

Gizmo

Another word for a gadget.

Grigio

Italian for "grey,"

Gus

Short for Augustus, as in Augustus the Great – the first

emperor of ancient Rome.

Gus

A Disney cat name inspired by the mouse from "Cinderella."

Hagrid

The giant caretaker of Hogwarts in the "Harry Potter" series.

Harley

This is a cool cat name in honour of Harley Davidson motorcycles.

Harry

Name your cat after the hero of the series, "Harry Potter." Also UK Prince Harry.

Hazel

Hazel is thought to come from the Old English word meaning a light brown colour.

Hermes

Percy Weasley's owl ("Harry Potter") can also turn into a name for your cat

Hermione

One of Harry Potter's best and smartest friends at Hogwarts.

Hobbes

In the comic strip "Calvin and Hobbes," Hobbes is Calvin's stuffed tiger.

Hot Wheels

Why not name your cat after your favourite childhood toy? There are no rules when it comes to cat naming!

Houdini

Like the famous magician, your cat may be a master of the disappearing act.

Indigo

This name can refer to your Siamese cat's lilac-tinged fur or those beautiful blue eyes.

Inky

The name connotes darkness, like your cat's dark fur.

Ivory

Another word for the white keys on the piano.

Izzy

Izzy can be short for Isabel, Isabella or Isadora.

Jack

A simple, sturdy name, whether as a nickname for Jackson or to the actor Jack Nicholson.

Jackie

An endearing nickname for Jack or Jacqueline.

Jackson

Jackson literally means "son of Jack," but you could also pick this male cat name inspired by Jackson Pollock, the abstract painter.

Jade

This green stone was originally found in China, Southeast Asia and India, and

would be a great Siamese cat name.

Jake

used to mean "OK" a century ago when your grandparents (or great-grandparents) were using slang.

Jamie

James might be too formal a name for your pet, but Jamie has a relaxed tone to it.

Jasmine

A flower found in Thailand, and a very pretty name

for your female Siamese.

Jax

A nickname for Jackson.

Jet

Another synonym for "black,"

Jiji

The pet feline in the Japanese animated film, "Kiki's Delivery Service".

Jim Jum

What better way to honour your Siamese cat's

heritage than to name them after this Thai soup?

Joey

"Joseph" may be too formal of a name for a cat, but "Joey" is a more laid-back, cool cat name. And it's a unisex cat name, too!

Kali

If you are looking for a girl cat name, "Kali Cat" has a great ring to it.

Keanu

The cat featured in "Keanu," starring Jordan Peele and

Keegan-Michael Key.

Khaki

Another word that means cream or beige, Army coloured clothing which could be the color of your cat's fur.

King

In honor of their royal roots, give your Siamese cat a regal name.

Kit Kat

Description a Kit Kat is a delicious chocolate bar.

Kitten

Maybe not the most creative cat name, but it's a good choice for any cat parent who doesn't want their baby to grow up.

Kitty

Sure, it's another word for cat, but it's also a common nickname for Catherine or Katherine.

Kitty Purry

For all the Katy Perry fans out there.

Kobe

Koopa

Inspired by the dinosaur from Super Mario and just an all-around cool cat name.

Koosh Ball

Remember those soft and fluffy toys from your childhood years? Well, it's a unique cat name, too, perfect for fluffy, long-haired cats.

Lapis

A nod to your Siamese cat's blue eyes, as lapis lazuli is a blue stone.

Laranja

It is Portuguese for "orange," and if you're looking for a unique cat name, it fits the bill.

Latte

Coffee lovers, this is the name for your cat!

Layla

The name Layla is a girl's name of Arabic origin meaning "night," and a classic Eric Clapton song released in 1971.

Lazer

A cat name inspired by the curious personality of a cat who loves chasing laser beams.

Leche

The Spanish word for "milk."

Lemon

Do you have a bit of a sourpuss on your hands?

Leo

The name conjures up lions, the big cat-cousins of your new pet.

Lia

An alternative spelling to the name Leah, and one that will look pretty on your cat's tag.

Licorice

It's not the sweetest sweet around, but the colour of original black liquorice fits.

Lily

The flower is toxic to cats, but you can keep the blooms out of your home while still bestowing the name on your precious pet.

Litter Abner

"Loki

You may wonder why anybody would name their cat after a villain, but some Marvel fans will argue that Thor's brother is just misunderstood.

Lola

This is a popular baby name among celebrities like Annie Lennox.

Lollipop

A cat name inspired by her sweet personality.

Louie

This boy cat name means "famous warrior,"

Lucifer

The rather wicked cat from "Cinder ella."

Lucky

Lucy

This name means "light," but is also the name of the hilariously entertaining main character in "I Love Lucy."

Ludo

Ludo Bagman, a character in the "Harry Potter" books, is a wizard who works for the Ministry of Magic.

Luigi

The twin brother of Mario from the Super Mario Brothers franchise.

Luke

The most famous Luke is Luke Skywalker, making this a cool cat name for pet parents who are into "Star Wars."

Lulu

A female cat name that means "famous warrior," also LULU the British Singer.

Lumi

The word for "snow" in Finnish.

Luna

Spanish for "moon," which is a good name

Macaron

An ode to your favourite sweet treat, the French macaron.

Mack

Maggie

Magic

Favourite Magician

Malbec

Mali

The word for "jasmine" in Thai if you are looking for a pretty Siamese cat name.

Mango

This tropical fruit is orange on the inside and makes a sweet orange cat name for your new pet.

Marie

Berlioz and Toulouse's white-furred, pink-bowed sister in "The Aristocrats."

Marley

A cute cat name!

Marmalade

A slightly bitter jam made of oranges. Of course, your cat will be more sweet than bitter.

Marshmallow

A cat name reserved for the fluffiest, softest white kitties.

Max

Yes, it is a really popular name among pet parents, and for good reason: It means "greatest."

Maya

A cute cat name in honour of the poet Maya Angelou.

Meow Farrow

In honour of "Rosemary's Baby" actress Mia Farrow.

Meow Hamm

More of a sports fan? Choose this name as an homage to athlete Mia Hamm.

Merengue

Merengue is a type of music and dance popular throughout Latin America. So, if you love dancing to Latin music with your cat, this could be a unique cat name.

Merry

It is not just for Christmas! Use it when you are looking for different kitten names.

Mickey

Yes, Mickey Mouse is a rodent, not a cat, and that makes it a good cat name, too.

Midnight

A dark time of night, and a great black cat name!

Miles

A unique cat name if you're a runner.

Milky

It's a myth that cats need milk (though they'll drink it), but why not name your cat after it.

Millie

Mildred may be too formal of a cat name, but this nickname has a ring to it!

Milo

The feline sidekick from "The Adventures of Milo and Otis."

Mimi

Does your cat give off that "La Vie Boehme" vibe? Then name her after Mimi, the character from the musical "Rent."

Minerva

Minerva McGonagall is the Transfiguration teacher who can turn into a cat in the "Harry Potter" series.

Minnie

Probably one of the most classic Disney character names.

Missy

Melissa may not be that great of a cat name, but the shortened version, Missy, is super cute!

Misty

A mist, or fog, often looks grey, and according to a Carl Sandburg poem, "fog comes creeping on little cat feet."

Mittens

Fun fact: Mittens the cat is a local celebrity in Wellington, New Zealand

.

Mochi

The cat in "Big Hero 6."

Moose

Does your cat have a personality as big as a moose?

Mousse

A delicious name to celebrate the sweet addition to your home!

Mrs. Norris

The name of Argus Filch's cat in the "Harry Potter" series.

Muffin

Your favourite breakfast treat becomes an adorable name for your new pet.

Munchkin

Another cute moniker, especially if your cat is on the small side or a Munchkin cat breed.

Murphy

This name means "descendant of sea

warrior," a unique cat name for cats who don't mind getting a little wet.

Myrtle

In the "Harry Potter" series, Moaning Myrtle is the ghost that appears in the girls' bathroom.

Nacho

Who doesn't love nachos? Name your cat after one of the most beloved appetizers of all time.

Nala

Simba's female counterpart in "The Lion King."

Nazareth

The place where Joseph and Mary came from, and returned, after their baby's birth in Bethlehem.

Nermal

One of the characters from the "Garfield" series.

Nero

That's "black" in Italian, as well as an infamous Roman emperor.

Nick

In the "Harry Potter" series, Nearly Headless Nick is

the ghost that haunts Gryffindor.

Nico

You may want to name your cat Nico, short for Nicolas (or Nicholas), a name meaning "victory of the people."

Nugget

The cat's name for your sweet little nugget.

O'Malley

The surname of the street cat who falls in love with the Duchess in "The Artistocats."

Oliver

With origins in Old English and French, this name originally meant "olive tree planter."

Olivia

Ollie

Onyx

A gemstone that is known for its shiny black colour.

Opal

This milky white gem is October's traditional birthstone and is said to have healing powers.

Orca

This fierce whale is black and white,

and your cat is probably fierce, too (especially around mealtimes).

Oreo

These biscuits are black on the outside, white on the inside.

Oscar

Maybe your cat is a little grumpy sometimes, so you picked this tongue-in-cheek reference to Oscar the Grouch.

Pad

Means "fried" in Thai and is a word found in famous Thai dishes (like pad Thai).

Padma

The name of a Hogwarts student, Padma Patil, who attended the Yule Ball with Ron Weasley, Harry Potter, and her twin sister, Parvati.

Paloma

Spanish for "dove" (which can be gray or white), so a great girl cat name for your feminine feline.

Panda

If you want to name your black-and-white cat after another black-and-white animal and zebra just won't cut it, this cute bear might do the trick.

Papaya

Another tropical fruit that's reddish orange, and can be used as a girl cat name or a boy cat name.

Paw Paw

Named after paw paw plant

Peaches

Another orange-colored fruit that can be used as an orange cat name.

Peanut

A sweet unisex cat name for your adorable little peanut.

Peanut Butter

Maybe your cat is a perfect shade of peanut butter?

Pearl

A gemstone that's often white or cream coloured.

PeeWee

Penny

A shortened version of Penelope, which could also be a nice girl cat name.

Pepper

If you want a unique cat name inspired by his or her spicy personality, this is the one!

Peppo

The Italian alley cat in "The Aristocats."

Pickles

A little sweet, a little sour–just like your cat!

Pink

Short for Pink Panther.

Piper

A piper is a flute player, so maybe your cat likes to make music in the form of meowing.

Pippa

This name means "lover of horses"—good for a barn cat, perhaps?

Pisco

The national liquor in Chile and Peru can make for a unique cat name.

Pixie

These mythical beings are similar to elves, and are associated with cuteness (like the pixie cut).

Plata

The Spanish word for "silver."

Plato

Plato was a Greek philosopher, so if your cat seems exceptionally wise, this may be a fitting name.

Polly Pocket

A name inspired by the fun kids' toy. You can call her Polly for short!

Pop Tart

A loose Woman.

Popple

A Popple is a plush toy that transforms from a stuffed animal into a ball–

which may resemble how your cat sleeps.

Porgy

This fish-inspired name is funny and pretty at the same time (and also references "Porgy and Bess," the name of an opera by George Gershwin).

Prince

In humans, he is the son of the king. For your cat, he is the heir to your heart.

Princess

Meaning the daughter of a king or queen, this name has a pampered vibe.

Puffalump

Puffalumps were plush toys that originally appeared in the 1980s, but were eventually discontinued. However, you can still steal this cute cat name!

Puffin

Another black-and-white animal, not to be confused with penguins.

Pumpkin

Yes, you can name your tabby cat after this orange gourd, and it also fits cats who come into your life in the fall.

Pusheen

This cartoon cat is a tubby tabby who brings smiles and laughter to people all around the world.

Quince

These fruits are like apples and serve as a unisex name for both girls and boys.

Rain

Raindrops don't really have a colour, but the days accompanying rain are grey.

Rajah

The tiger in "Aladdin."

Raven

The bird that appears in Edgar Allen Poe's poem quoting "Nevermore," and known for its shiny black feathers.

Ravenclaw

The name of one of the four houses at Hogwarts in the "Harry Potter" series.

Remy

Does your cat love food? Consider naming them after the aspiring chef in the Disney movie "Ratatouille."

Riley

This lovely name comes from Ireland and means "courageous."

Rocky

For the cat that's as tough as the one-and-only Rocky Balboa.

Romeo

Is your cat the handsomest around? Name him Romeo!

Rose

Roses are associated with love, and so is your pet.

Roxie

Just like Rosie the Riveter, the World War II-era icon.

Roxie

Many Roxies (or Roxys) are actually Roxannes, but the name is from Persia and means "dawn," so it's a great fit for Persian cats.

Ruby

A ruby is a red stone often associated with power and wealth. It's the best cat name for the cat that is king or queen of your castle.

Rufus

The cat in "The Rescuers."

Ryder

It's a popular baby boy's name (and the name of Kate Hudson's son), but it's a great male cat name, too.

Sadie

Sadie means "princess." It's a lovely female cat name inspired by her personality!

Saffron

This herb gives a golden orange-yellow colour to foods when you cook with it, and certainly can be classified as a cool cat name.

Sagwa

The main character in the animated TV series, "Sagwa, the Chinese Siamese Cat."

Salem

The origin of the name Salem is Hebrew and means "peace."

Salmon Rushdie

A play on the name of author Salman Rushdie, and maybe your cat's favorite fish.

Sam

Don't you just want to pick this male cat name so you can call him "Sam the Man?"

Sammy

Sammy is a unisex cat name, short for either Samuel or Samantha.

Santa Claws

You don't have to call your cat by their full name. Just use Claws.

Sapphire

Another way of paying tribute to your cat's gorgeous baby blues.

Sasha

This name is often used as a nickname for Alexandra and Natasha.

Sassy

The cat starring in "Homeward Bound: The Incredible Journey" (and voiced by Sally Field).

Scabbers

The name of Ron Weasley's pet rat in the "Harry Potter" series.

Scout

The name may be reminiscent of the Boy Scouts, but it can actually be a unisex cat name. Bruce Willis and Demi Moore named their daughter Scout.

Scratchmo

A play on "Satchmo," the nickname for jazz great Louis Armstrong.

Shadow

A great black cat name for those who follow you around the house.

Shakira

Named after the Colombian singer Shakira, whose "Hips Don't Lie."

Shortcake

Shortcake is a dessert with just the right amount of sweet.

Silver

A classy way of honouring your cat's fur colour, and an excellent grey cat name.

Simba

This name belongs to the cocky cub who grows into the titular character in "The Lion King."

Sirius

Sirius Black was Harry Potter's godfather, so this is a great boy cat name for a black kitty.

Sky

An homage to your kitty's baby blue eyes.

Smokey

We know you will not be smoking around your cat (it's bad for them), but you can certainly give them a name that calls up the colour Gray.

Snape

One of Hogwarts' most famous teachers is Severus Snape, Harry Potter's nemesis.

Snickers

Sweet on the outside and a little nutty on the inside!

Snowbell

The white Persian cat in "Stuart Little.

Snowy

If you get your new pet in the winter, this may make a

good white cat name!

Socks

Bill and Hilary Clinton's pet cat during their time in the White House.

Socrates

Socrates was a Greek philosopher known for being one of the founders of Western philosophy.

Soda Pop

A cat name inspired by your cat's bubbly personality.

Sofia

Alternately spelled Sophia, this is

originally a Greek name meaning "wisdom," and really, there is nothing wiser than a cat.

Sonic

Name your cat after this super fast, super cool video game character.

Sonora

A Mexican state that may strike your fancy.

Sophie

Meaning "wisdom," this is a great girl cat name for your wise fur baby.

Spooky

Stella

The name means "star," and your felines more than ready for her leading role in your life.

Stimpson

"Stimpy" for short, he's the co-star of "The Ren & Stimpy Show."

Stormy

Stormy days are gray, so this may be just the right gray cat name for your kitty.

Sugar

It's white and sweet, just like your new kitten.

Sundae

A sweet treat of ice cream smothered in a topping such as chocolate sauce.

Sunny

A girl or boy cat name inspired by their sunny personality!

Sunshine

For the cat who never fails to bring a little sunshine to your day.

Sushi

For the cat who loves any type of fish.

Sylvester

This black-and-white cat from the old "Looney Tunes" cartoons was constantly being outwitted by Tweety bird.

Taffy

A sweet found on beach boardwalks, and great name for a girl cat.

Tamagotchi

Your first pet may have been a Tamagotchi, but now you've upgraded to the real thing. This unisex cat name is a throwback to your younger years preparing to be a pet parent.

Tartlet

A tartlet is a small pastry and a unique cat name for a tiny, sweet kitty.

Tawny

Traditional Siamese cats have cream- or tawny-coloured fur, as well as feet and paws.

Teddy

Do you want to snuggle with your cat like your favourite teddy bear? Name him Teddy!

Teddy Ruxpin

Named after the talking toy teddy bear that loves to tell stories.

Tessa

You can use this version for your cat or take off the "a" and name her Tess.

Theo

Theo means "divine gift," which is exactly what your cat is!

Thor

Thor is the Norse god of thunder, a fitting name for any cat who loves a good thunderstorm.

Tibbs

Sergeant Tibbs helped Pongo and Perdita rescue their pups in "101 Dalmatians."

Tiger

After the exotic tiger?

Tigger

The bouncy, orange tiger in "Winnie the Pooh" movies and books might describe your lovely cat.

Tiny Tim

If your furball is on the smallish side, you can't go wrong with this name from Charles Dickens' "A Christmas Carol."

Toby

Toby is a popular name that comes from Tobias.

Todd

This name means "fox," which could be a funny cat name for an orange cat with pointy ears.

Tofu

This white food is perfect for your cat's name, even though they would never touch it!

Tonto

The feline sidekick in "Harry and Tonto."

Totoro

Totoro is an adorable chinchilla from a Japanese animated film called "My Neighbour Totoro." You can call your cat Toto for short!

Toulouse

The orange kitten and oldest child of Duchess in "The aristocats."

Trevor

The name of Neville Longbottom's pet toad in the "Harry Potter" series.

Trixie

Short for Beatrix, the name comes from Latin and means "she who brings happiness.

Tucker
You can call him "Tuck" for short!

Turnip

Sure, a turnip is a root vegetable, but it can be a cute cat name!

Tuxedo

This black-and-white formal attire makes an elegant black-and-white cat name.

Twix

A cat name inspired
by a CHOCOLAT
BAR.

Ursula

The sea witch in
"The Little
Mermaid."

Venus

Venus is the
goddess of love,
the best cat's name
for an extra
loveable cat.

Violet

Some Siamese
cats have a violet
tinge to their pale
fur and are actually
called lilac point
Siamese.

Wahoo

The name of a fish,
or an excited
exclamation!

Walter

If your cat is white,
you can name him
Walter White, from
the TV show
"Breaking Bad."

Whiskey

This name can
serve as a shorter
form of Whiskers.

Whispurr

A play on whisper,
but you can call
your cat Wispy for
short.

Willow

While Willow is usually a girl cat name, it can make for a cool boy cat name.

Winifred Sanderson

One of the witches in the movie "Hocus Pocus," played by Bette Midler.

Wolfgang Amadeus Mouse-art

Beloved of God, A pun based on composer Wolfgang Amadeus Mozart.

Yoggi

Is a person who has spent many years practicing the philosophy of yoga.

Yoshi

Inspired by the dinosaur from Super Mario and just an all-around cool cat name.

Zack, Zach or Zac

Zeke

Some experts think cats respond best to "ee" sounds, making this name a tactical choice.

Zelda

Zelda Fitzgerald was the "It girl" in the 1920s

Ziggy

Ziggy means "victorious

protector" and the best cat name for any cat that feels he has to protect your house.

Zoe

The name means "life" in Greek.

Printed in Great Britain
by Amazon